THE GOD AROUND US

A Child's Garden of Prayer

Mira Pollak Brichto

Illustrated by Selina Alko

Revised Edition

UAHC Press
New York

To my mother
Riza Fleischman Pollak
who taught me prayer
MPB

To my grandparents
Molly and Daniel
SA

Library of Congress Cataloging-in-Publication Data
Brichto, Mira Pollak.
The God around us: a child's garden of prayer/Mira Pollak
Brichto; illustrated by Selina Alko.—Rev. ed.
p.   cm.
  Includes blessings in Hebrew, romanized Hebrew, and English translation.
  Summary: Simple poems are paired with prayers in Hebrew and English.
ISBN 0-8074-07-1-1
1. Jewish children Prayer-books and devotions—English.
2. Jewish children Prayer-books and devotions—Hebrew.
3. Judaism Prayer-books and devotions—English.
4. Judaism Prayer-books and devotions—Hebrew.
[1. Judaism Prayer-books and devotions. 2. Hebrew language materials—
Bilingual.]
I. Alko, Selina, ill.
II. Title.
BM666.B7 1999
296.4'5—dc21   99-17465
                                                    CIP

Book design by Itzhack Shelomi
Manufactured in the United States of America

10 9 8 7 6 5 4 3 2 1

Foreword

Children love to pray. They pray naturally, spontaneously, and gracefully—if adults let them—and how much more if parents help them. For prayer is the expression of our deepest emotions (joy, sorrow, desire, wonder, gratitude) in the meaningful context of a God around us.

This picture book of poems and prayers (adapted from centuries-old Jewish formulae) is meant to be a guide for parent and child—pointing out the wondrous experiences of everyday life and crystalizing out of them something concrete that will remain with the child forever: the majesty of the ocean, mountains, falling stars, and thunder; the beauty of a rainbow or a flower; gratitude for food or a loved one's return; the joy of good tidings or the sorrow of bereavement.

The poems and prayers should be read and reread until they become the common property of parent and child. Then many an actual experience will evoke the poems and prayers from memory and thus provide for the wholehearted expression of feelings as meaningful as they are fleeting.

It is our hope that the child will gain a familiarity with the prayer experience itself through a learning process that is warm, intimate, and unself-conscious; and that such a bond will be forged between parent and child as can come only from the sharing of some of life's thrilling and holy moments.

Mira Pollak Brichto

A mountain high, a falling star,
These things to me a wonder are.
The lightning sky, the desert sand,
Let's praise the work of God's own hand.

Praised are You, Adonai our God, Ruler of the universe,
who performs the work of creation.

בָּרוּךְ אַתָּה יְיָ אֱלֹהֵינוּ מֶלֶךְ הָעוֹלָם,
עֹשֶׂה מַעֲשֵׂה בְּרֵאשִׁית.

*Baruch Atah Adonai Eloheinu Melech ha'olam,
oseh ma'aseh bereshit.*

Frozen ground begins to break,
Sleeping roots push up and wake.
Weeping willow, apple, pear,
Tender blossoms everywhere.

Praised are You, Adonai our God, Ruler of the universe,
for wonderful creations and trees to delight humankind.

בָּרוּךְ אַתָּה יְיָ אֱלֹהֵינוּ מֶלֶךְ הָעוֹלָם,
אֲשֶׁר בָּרָא בְּעוֹלָמוֹ בְּרִיּוֹת טוֹבוֹת וְאִילָנוֹת טוֹבִים,
לְהָנוֹת בָּהֶם בְּנֵי אָדָם.

Baruch Atah Adonai Eloheinu Melech ha'olam,
asher bara be'olamo beriyot tovot ve'ilanot tovim,
lehanot bahem benei adam.

Friendly fingers push our bell
When neighbors have good news to tell,
Of weddings, birth—of girl or boy.
How good it is to share our joy!

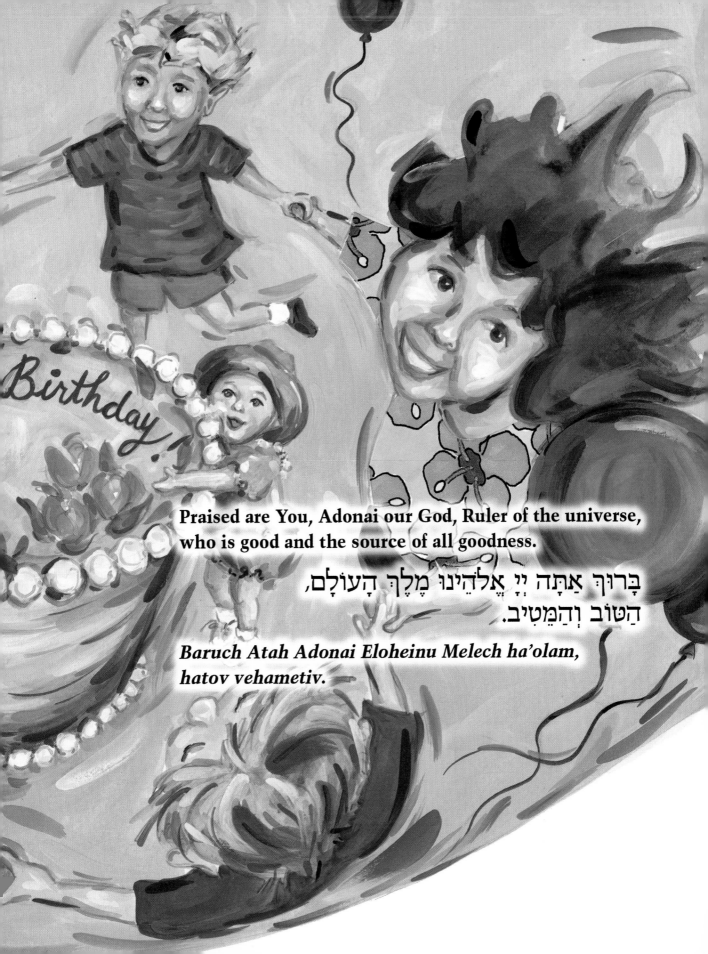

Praised are You, Adonai our God, Ruler of the universe, who is good and the source of all goodness.

בָּרוּךְ אַתָּה יְיָ אֱלֹהֵינוּ מֶלֶךְ הָעוֹלָם,
הַטּוֹב וְהַמֵּטִיב.

*Baruch Atah Adonai Eloheinu Melech ha'olam,
hatov vehametiv.*

Shining sun and falling rain,
Seed and soil make golden grain.
Oats and barley, rye and wheat
Spring from earth that all may eat.

Praised are You, Adonai our God, Ruler of the universe, who brings bread forth from the earth.

בָּרוּךְ אַתָּה יְיָ אֱלֹהֵינוּ מֶלֶךְ הָעוֹלָם,
הַמּוֹצִיא לֶחֶם מִן הָאָרֶץ:

*Baruch Atah Adonai Eloheinu Melech ha'olam,
hamotzi lechem min ha'aretz.*

Colors, tones, and shades of skin,
Black and brown and white are kin.
Whether our color be dark or fair,
The same red blood alike we share.

Praised are You, Adonai our God, Ruler of the universe,
who varies the creatures.

בָּרוּךְ אַתָּה יְיָ אֱלֹהֵינוּ מֶלֶךְ הָעוֹלָם, מְשַׁנֶּה הַבְּרִיּוֹת.

*Baruch Atah Adonai Eloheinu Melech ha'olam,
meshaneh habriyot.*

Older than mountain, bluer than sky,
The ocean rolls before my eye.
The God who made the deep blue sea
Will always treasure you and me.

Praised are You, Adonai our God, Ruler of the universe,
who made the great sea.

בָּרוּךְ אַתָּה יְיָ אֱלֹהֵינוּ מֶלֶךְ הָעוֹלָם,
שֶׁעָשָׂה אֶת הַיָּם הַגָּדוֹל.

Baruch Atah Adonai Eloheinu Melech ha'olam,
she'asah et hayam hagadol.

The storm has passed. The sun is high.
A bridge of rainbow climbs the sky:
God's pledge to Noah that the rain
Will never flood the world again.

Praised are You, Adonai our God, Ruler of the universe,
who in remembrance of the covenant faithfully
fulfills promises.

בָּרוּךְ אַתָּה יְיָ אֱלֹהֵינוּ מֶלֶךְ הָעוֹלָם,
זוֹכֵר הַבְּרִית וְנֶאֱמָן בִּבְרִיתוֹ וְקַיָּם בְּמַאֲמָרוֹ.

*Baruch Atah Adonai Eloheinu Melech ha'olam, zocher
haberit vene'eman biverito vekayam bema'amaro.*

Oftentimes we wonder why
All lovely living things must die.
We grieve and try to understand
Both life and death are in God's hand.

Praised are You, Adonai our God, Ruler of the universe,
the true Judge.

בָּרוּךְ אַתָּה יְיָ אֱלֹהֵינוּ מֶלֶךְ הָעוֹלָם, דַּיַּן הָאֱמֶת.

Baruch Atah Adonai Eloheinu Melech ha'olam,
Dayan ha'emet.

Potatoes do not grow French fried,
Mashed, or baked with butter inside.
But raw we find them in the ground,
Where carrots, squash, and beets abound.

Praised are You, Adonai our God, Ruler of the universe, who creates the fruit of the earth.

בָּרוּךְ אַתָּה יְיָ אֱלֹהֵינוּ מֶלֶךְ הָעוֹלָם,
בּוֹרֵא פְּרִי הָאֲדָמָה.

*Baruch Atah Adonai Eloheinu Melech ha'olam,
borei peri ha'adamah.*

Children listen everywhere,
As rumbling thunder fills the air.
In storm by night or storm by day,
We fear not, as to God we pray.

Praised are You, Adonai our God, Ruler of the universe, whose power and might fills the world.

בָּרוּךְ אַתָּה יְיָ אֱלֹהֵינוּ מֶלֶךְ הָעוֹלָם,
שֶׁכֹּחוֹ וּגְבוּרָתוֹ מָלֵא עוֹלָם.

*Baruch Atah Adonai Eloheinu Melech ha'olam,
shekocho ugevurato malei olam.*

There's nothing in the world so nice
As all the smells of flowers and spice.
Jasmine, ginger, lilac, rose,
How your fragrance tickles my nose.

Praised are You, Adonai our God, Ruler of the universe,
who creates fragrant flowers and herbs.

בָּרוּךְ אַתָּה יְיָ אֱלֹהֵינוּ מֶלֶךְ הָעוֹלָם,
בּוֹרֵא עִשְׂבֵי בְשָׂמִים.

Baruch Atah Adonai Eloheinu Melech ha'olam,
borei isvei vesamim.

A hug, a kiss, an outstretched hand
As ships return and airplanes land.
Father, mother, cousin, friend,
Welcome home at journey's end.

Praised are You, Adonai our God, Ruler of the universe,
who returns loved ones safely home.

בָּרוּךְ אַתָּה יְיָ אֱלֹהֵינוּ מֶלֶךְ הָעוֹלָם, מְחַיֵּה הַמֵּתִים.

Baruch Atah Adonai Eloheinu Melech ha'olam,
mechayeh hametim.

Traditional Uses of the Blessings in This Volume

1. *...ma'aseh bereshit.*

Traditionally recited upon seeing a natural phenomenon, such as lightning, mountains, and rivers.

2. *...asher bara be'olamo beriyot tovot ve'ilanot tovim lehanot bahem benei adam..*

Traditionally recited when seeing a fruit tree blossom for the first time in the year.

3. *...hatov vehametiv.*

Traditionally recited upon hearing good news.

4. *...hamotzi lechem min ha'aretz.*

Traditionally recited before eating bread made from wheat, barley, rye, oats, or spelt.

5. *...meshaneh habriyot.*

Traditionally recited when seeing people of different races and may also be used upon seeing uniquely formed people, such as dwarfs and giants.

6. *...she'asah et hayam hagadol.*

Traditionally recited when seeing the ocean.

7. *...zocher haberit vene'eman biverito vekayam bema'amaro.*

Traditionally recited when seeing a rainbow, which (according to the story of Noah in Genesis) is a sign of God's promise that the earth will never again be destroyed by a flood.

8. ...*Dayan ha'emet.*

   Traditionally recited upon hearing bad news, during *keriah*, the tearing or cutting that precedes a funeral.

9. ...*borei peri ha'adamah.*

   Traditionally recited before eating fruits and vegetables that specifically grow in the ground. Other blessings are used for produce that grows on vines or on trees.

10. ...*shekocho ugevurato malei olam.*

    Traditionally recited when hearing thunder.

11. ...*borei isvei vesamim.*

    Traditionally recited when smelling flowers or herbs.

12. ...*mechayeh hametim.*

    Recited upon greeting travelers returning from perilous journeys, this is the closing line of the second section of the daily prayer, the *Amidah*. This section is known as the *Gevurot*. Traditionally the *Gevurot* testifies to God's ability to save us no matter what our physical or spiritual condition.

Acknowledgments

I want to acknowledge a debt greater than I feel I can express to Abraham N. Franzblau, who first saw, critiqued, and encouraged this effort; to Eugene B. Borowitz, who with an interest compounded of warm generosity and firm patience would not accept the good—if there were the possibility of better; to Chaim Stern, who put the new wine of fresh interpretation into the old bottle of מִשְׁנֶה הַבְּרִיּוֹת; to Chanan and Sidney Brichto, who in recollection of laughter and tears share with me the knowledge of the mountainous labor that goes into a four-line verse; to Eric H. Yoffie, who knew the time for this reissue had arrived.

Mira Pollak Brichto